GMP

Good Manufacturing Practices

Carlos H Hernández

GMP

Practical Guide

First Edition in English, 2018

Series: Management System

COPYRIGHT Carlos H Hernández

ISBN-13: 978-1792901430

Content

Introduction 10
What are the GMP? 11
Structure 11
    Establishment 13
    Operational Practices 13
    Surveillance 14
Guidelines for Good Manufacturing Practices 15
    Infrastructure 15
    Layout and workspace 15
    Utilities 16
    Waste Disposal 19
    Equipment suitability, cleaning and maintenance 20
    Management of purchased materials and services 22
    Measures for prevention of contamination 23
    Cleaning 25
    Pest control 26
    Personnel hygiene and facilities 28
    Rework 30
    Withdrawal procedures 30
    Storage and transport 31
    Food packaging information and customer communication 33
    Food defense and bioterrorism 33
Example of checklist and monitoring of compliance with GMP 34
Glossary 39
References 40

Introduction.

Nowadays the organizations of all the sectors of the economy, have as goal to increase their efficiency in all their processes. Reduce waste is a way that brings significant savings to organizations and therefore their profits are increased. The Good Manufacturing Practices or Good Operating Practices, to call them in a more generic way, are a set of tools that help to identify the risks and therefore control them in order to reduce the negative impacts that may cause deviations in the processes and, as result in products or services that do not comply with the established requirements. These deviations in the processes are the causes of the waste.

The GMP (Good Manufacturing Practices) as we will call them in this text, help to create awareness in the personnel that participate in the elaboration of the products or services; they generate a preventive culture and discipline and thus organizations can anticipate possible deviations from the processes. The standardization of the practices achieved through continuous improvement has resulted in the general acceptance of GMP.

The food industry and the packaging industry have compliance with GMP as mandatory, in accordance with their productive sector. These requirements vary according to the sector, but here I present a general structure that can be applied to most productive sectors. Not necessarily only these two types of industries must implement GMP, but any organization that seeks to gain efficiency in their processes, improve their quality system or management systems in general, control risks, standardize their operating practices, among others.

The 5S methodology and the GMP work together in the organization, both facilitate what is required by both parties and prepare the organization to have a lighter, more manageable, concise, understandable HACCP plan (Hazard Analysis and Critical Control Points), refined and reliable. Both constitute a strong mandatory prerequisite of the HACCP plan.

The GMP controls and monitors the policies and guidelines of the operation, prevents the before and after the productive line or services, in addition to establishing preventive behaviors, while the HACCP controls are specific in safety.

GMPs have become a bulwark in food processing, which is why all governments legislate creating laws, decrees that guarantee that the industry implements and complies.

The FDA (Food and Drug Administration) in its guideline 21 CFR regulates the content of GMP for the following industries: food, pharmaceutical, blood collection, medical equipment and animal medicine.

What are the GMP?

A good practice is to adhere to a methodology, system, tool or proven technique whose results have been outstanding and recognized. Good practices are standardized and extrapolated to other processes.

The GMP are basic principles and general practices of hygiene in the person, handling, preparation, processing, packaging, storage, transportation and distribution of food, drugs, packaging and products for human and animal consumption to ensure that they are safe, healthy and innocuous.

We can say that GMP is a preventive system that ensures the proper design, monitoring and control of manufacturing processes and facilities. It includes the establishment of quality management systems throughout the process from the procurement of materials to the delivery of products and services to customers. This formal system of controls helps to prevent cases of contamination, confusion, deviations, failures and errors.

Its importance is based on working methods, machinery and equipment, facilities and controls in production processes. They ensure the quality of the processes including packaging and labeling.

Structure.

In the Food Safety Management Systems the GMP is known as Pre-Requisite Programs (PRP), they work as the basis of the safety system, they must be implemented throughout the food chain (organizations involved) regardless of their size or the complexity of their operations.

Structure of **F**ood **S**afety **M**anagement **S**ystem

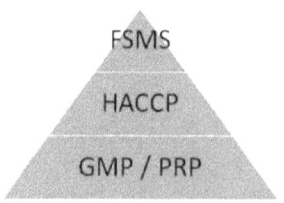

Policies, Processes, Documents, Audits

Hazard Analysis and Critical Control Points

Good Manufacturing Practices

Let's see the importance of GMP, they are the fundamental basis of a Food Safety Management System, as mentioned; they are a structure that supports the good performance of organizations because of their preventive nature. We must not forget that GMP are practices that create discipline in organizations.

The PRP take different names according to the sector where the organization is, examples of which are GMP (Good Manufacturing Practices), GHP (Good Hygienic Practices), GAP (Good Agricultural Practices), GDP (Good Distribution Practices), GLP (Good Laboratory Practices), etc.

The GMP, being the central axis of a food safety management system, must cover the sensitive areas of an organization, areas that can be decisive to avoid failures or deviations in the processes. In general, GMP should cover the following: personnel practices, establishment and work spaces, waste management and pest control, water and air services, cleaning practices and equipment maintenance, storage and transport, measures for the prevention of contamination, purchased materials and control of suppliers, re-works, recalls of products from the market, action in emergencies, information on products and communication with the customer, food defense, bio-surveillance and bio-terrorism.

Very important is the periodic monitoring of compliance with GMP. The frequency is defined by each organization.

Scheme of the GMP

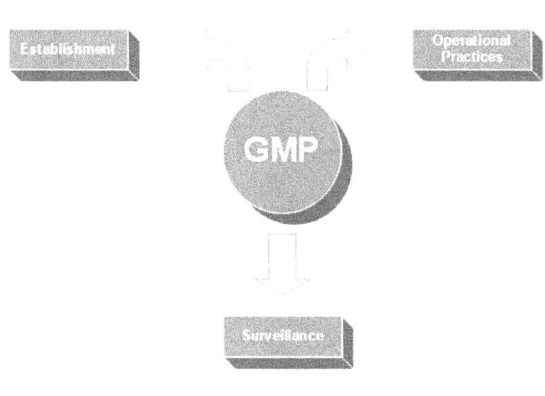

Establishment.

All the facilities of the organization must provide the security and confidence that the personnel, processes and conditions will not introduce dangers for the safety of the products. Its design must be in accordance with the requirements of the operation when receiving, moving, storing, transporting, handling or processing raw materials and supplies, as well as handling, storage and shipment of the finished product.

In this section we must focus on the:

- → Infrastructure,
- → Distribution of the operation and workspaces and
- → Services used by the operation.

Operational Practices.

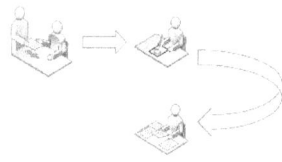
Operational and Personnel Practices methods that show how a facility can prevent people and processes from contaminating a product. The methods of cleaning, sanitization and disinfection, types of chemical products used, frequency of cleaning activities and control of microorganisms, must be according to the type of organization and the nature of its operations.

Operational practices or OPRP must be carried out in an ideal way to protect the products from issues related to their food safety, they must provide the guidelines to prevent contamination, to optimize the design and care of the installation and equipment, in order to make them easy to handle and not cause problems of health or safety of the products. They also provide multi-pronged strategies that ensure that pests or waste do not adulterate food or packaging. The prerequisite programs are specific to the needs of each organization.

The operational practices to be taken into account in this section are:

- Waste disposal,
- Equipment suitability, cleaning and maintenance,
- Management of purchased materials and services,
- Measures for prevention of contamination,
- Cleaning,

- Pest Control,
- Personnel hygiene and facilities,
- Rework,
- Withdrawal procedures and
- Storage and transport.

The main difference between a prerequisite program and an operational prerequisite program is that the operational prerequisites are born as such from the hazard analysis and are part of the process line and the prerequisite program are programs that allow us to maintain a safety environment, to ensure that the product that is manufactured within the process lines will be safe. In short, they are our first barrier to control the risks or dangers inherent in the process.

Surveillance.

Efforts should be made to protect the products from intentional acts of adulteration. The organization must ensure that the materials used are from secure sources and ensure access to all facilities, periodically evaluating the effectiveness of its surveillance system. Special emphasis should be placed on:

- ☑ Food packaging information and customer communication and
- ☑ Food defense and bioterrorism.

By implementing and maintaining all of these guidelines, organizations are controlling the points that can put at risk the operation of the organization. These guidelines must be known by all members of the organization, they must be audited (audits and self-inspections are a mandatory tool in continuous improvement) and corrected non-conformities detected. They provide a systematic and proactive approach that allows the permanent identification of risks and the development of control measures.

Guidelines for Good Manufacturing Practices.

Infrastructure.

The infrastructure of the establishment must have the appropriate characteristics to house the product or service, it must be able to minimize the risks detected in an initial analysis. It is necessary to carry out an initial analysis that serves to identify and control all the risks, vulnerabilities and threats with negative impacts that may originate from the infrastructure and its surroundings. Once the methodology of this analysis has been implemented, it should be carried out at least once a year and should remain as documented information.

> It is necessary to carry out an initial analysis that serves to identify and control all the risks, vulnerabilities and threats with negative impacts that may originate from the infrastructure and its surroundings.

After corrections to the state of the infrastructure, corrective actions have been developed.

The characteristics of the infrastructure must mainly have buildings that must be manufactured with a durable construction according to the type of product or service, but in general, emphasis should be placed on: the boundaries of the installation must be clearly defined, consider all sources of contamination that may come from external areas, the good condition of roofs, walls, floors, drains, elevated structures, temporary and mobile structures, windows, doors, loading and unloading docks, roads, gardens and parking areas.

Layout and workspace.

The distribution in plant implies the ordering of necessary spaces for movement of material, storage, equipment or lines of production, industrial equipment, direct and indirect work teams, administration, services for the personnel and all the activities that take place in the organization.

> Generally, a good flow facilitates good hygiene and operational practices of the organization. A good distribution also takes into account the waste movements of the processes, which can cause cross contamination.

The reduction of risks of occupational diseases, accidents at work, cross contamination; it is contemplated from the design and it is a vital vision from the distribution of the operations, in this way the obstacles in the corridors are eliminated; dangerous steps, reduces the likelihood of slips, unhealthy places, poor ventilation, poor lighting, poor flow of materials and products; in other words, the operational flow is improved.

Generally, a good flow facilitates good hygiene and operational practices of the organization. A good distribution also takes into account the waste movements of the processes, which can cause cross contamination.

The distribution of operations should not be something static, rather it should be considered to change it when operations, maintenance, cleaning, storage are difficult, when potential contamination hazards are detected, as new methods of work are introduced, introducing new processes to the process products or services, when making changes in machinery and equipment locations, after having made an analysis that the distribution increases the waste, re process or rework, etc.

Utilities.

The provision of support services and their distribution routes in and around the process or storage areas should be designed to prevent the risk of product contamination. The quality of service supplies must be monitored to prevent any risk of product contamination.

The most used services are: water, compressed air, steam, fuels, other gases and lighting. . All services must meet the requirements stipulated in their supply contract. These service providers must be evaluated periodically and, if possible, they must be audited by the organization with an established and planned program.

The supply of drinking water must be sufficient for the needs of the production process. The storage and distribution facilities, and when applicable, of temperature control, must be designed to meet the specified quality requirements for water. It is also imperative that drinking water complies with WHO requirements for drinking water or local regulations.

The water used as an ingredient, including that used to make ice or steam, (including culinary steam), or that in contact with the product or with the surfaces in contact with the product must be of the quality and microbiological requirements relevant to the product.

When chlorinated water supplies are used, checks shall be made of the appropriate level of chlorination, which, as specified, ensures the permanence of residual chlorine within the established limits.

Non-potable water must have separate pipes and cannot be mixed by interconnection or reflux with potable water.

Regarding air quality, the organization must establish the requirements for filtering, % relative humidity and microbial load of the air used as an ingredient or that comes into direct contact with the product.

Proper ventilation should be provided for the removal of excess undesirable vapor, dust or odors and to facilitate drying after wet cleaning. The amount of air renewal varies according to the established process. In general, organizations must use natural or forced ventilation systems. In this way, it is necessary to make a number of renewals every hour depending on the volume to be ventilated, taking into account not only the number of workers, but the size of the industrial area should be one of the most important aspects to be taken into account.

Natural ventilation

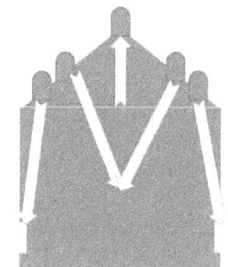

Forced Ventilation with Injection and Natural Air Extraction

When there is a risk of contamination by air, the microbiological quality of the air must be controlled. In the places where they are exposed to air pollution, products that can support the growth or survival of microbes, protocols must be in place to monitor and control air quality.

Systems should be constructed so that no air flows from dirty areas to clean areas. Defined pressure differentials must be maintained, preferably positive pressure in the process areas.

The systems must be accessible for cleaning, filter changes and maintenance. Filters for air in contact with food and packaging must be sanitary filters; Sanitary is a condition that is often confused with sterile. (Sterile means no bacteria or other living microorganisms present.) According to the FDA's Title 21 CFR provision, sterile air causes no microorganisms to pass with a challenge rate of 107 per cm^2). A sanitary filter is designed and constructed in a way that inhibits the growth of bacteria. All contact surfaces of the filter housing can be cleaned and users can easily disassemble the housing for inspection or cleaning. Sanitary filter housings are manufactured with materials that can be cleaned and prevent products from becoming contaminated. Manufacturers are based on industrial organizations, such as 3-A, that determine and define sanitary standards.

The protections of the external air intakes should be examined periodically to verify their physical integrity.

Gas systems such as compressed air, carbon dioxide, nitrogen or other gases used in production or packaging must be constructed and maintained to prevent contamination.

The gases used in direct or incidental contact with the product such as transportation, blowing, drying of products or equipment must be from an approved source and filtered to remove dust, oil and water.

> The air quality classes are defined according to ISO 8573-1: 2010, specifying the purity classes of the compressed air with respect to particles, water and oil, regardless of the location in the compressed air system in which specifies or measures the air.

When oil is used in the compressors and there is potential for air contact with the product, the used oil must be food grade. The filtering, moisture and microbiological specifications should be established.

Oil-free compressed air can only be achieved by installing an oil-free air compressor. Even so, it will still be necessary to filter the particles and remove the moisture.

The air quality classes are defined according to ISO 8573-1: 2010, specifying the purity classes of the compressed air with respect to particles, water and oil, regardless of the location in the compressed air system in which specifies or measures the air. The food and pharmaceutical industry must pay close attention to the quality of the compressed air that comes into contact with the products.

The lighting provided, natural or artificial, should allow the personnel to operate in a hygienic manner. The luminous intensity in each job depends on the nature of the position and must be measured and evaluated by competent personnel.

The lamps must be protected to avoid contamination of materials, products or equipment in case of cracks.

It is recommended to have a program of inspection and cleaning of the lamps and their protections.

The control and supervision of services is vital to eliminate the risk of cross contamination.

Waste Disposal.

The waste generated in all processes of organizations are produced in the processes of manufacturing, processing and use of inputs. These wastes must be handled correctly so that they are not a source of contamination. Organizations must identify, collect, remove and dispose of all waste in order to prevent contamination.

> Organizations must identify, collect, remove and dispose of all waste in order to prevent contamination.

Waste containers should be emptied at appropriate frequencies and kept in proper cleaning condition.

They should be away from the areas of production and storage of products and materials. Containers that are not for waste should not be confused, meaning that identification is vital to avoid confusion that may cause cross contamination.

The providers of the waste collection service must be trained in the management and final disposal. Have the permits that allow it to operate and the organization must ensure how and where the waste is disposed. Important to make sure that the commercial badges are destroyed in order to avoid possible misunderstandings with logos and brands.

For the identification of waste, many nomenclatures can be used, but basically the minimum information that must be stipulated is: Process that generates it, Type of waste (Dangerous and No-Dangerous), Quantity.

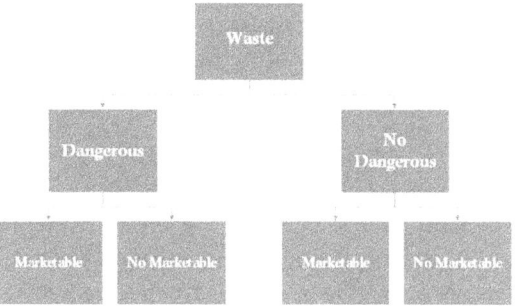

The most common faults in the handling of waste is the lack of identification, the non-segregation of the same and unopened containers.

Drains and water channels should be constructed in such a way that they facilitate their maintenance and cleaning, and are not points where waste is capable of accumulating preventing a potential source of contamination.

Equipment suitability, cleaning and maintenance.

The maintenance of machinery and equipment of the organization, is vital to achieve the production of safe food and to ensure that the products are manufactured according to specifications.

The training of maintenance personnel should be considered a high priority and be controlled by those holding senior management positions. Many times the maintenance is seen without the importance it deserves, when in reality the quality and the training of the personnel that carries out these activities must be given great importance.

> In other words, maintenance must be scheduled in order to ensure that activities are carried out in a planned manner

The maintenance of each of the machines or structures of the company in which they must carry under a certain schedule. In other words, the maintenance must be scheduled, in order to achieve that the activities are carried out in a planned manner and with the existence of spare parts so that it can be carried out without setbacks. There must be spare parts available so that production does not stop without being programmed. All spare parts that come into contact with food will be stored in a clean, elevated floor environment.

It is also important to give traceability to the activities carried out, it is necessary to achieve this purpose to manage and administer a log of maintenance operations that records the activities carried out; can contain the following information: Why stopped the machine, what was done, what parts were used, day, time, who was responsible for the activities, who received the machine or equipment after the repair was made.

The lubrication of machinery and equipment, depends on the machine used, the lubricants must be food grade in the parts that there is a risk of contact with the product. The fact of using food-grade lubricants does not mean that the conditions that may cause the contamination of these lubricants to the products should be neglected. The food grade lubricants are manufactured for occasional contaminations, not for recurrent and far from permanent. In the place where lubricants are stored in general, food grade lubricants must be located where there is no risk of contamination.

A planned maintenance system must be implemented for all equipment. The maintenance must be systematically carried out for the potential contamination produced by the equipment. Where there is a food safety risk, maintenance should be a priority. After each maintenance, it must be ensured that the equipment is free of contaminants and risks that may cause contamination. Maintenance personnel and subcontracted companies must follow all hygienic measures to avoid contamination. Special care will be taken with the used and chemical tools used.

Temporary repairs should be avoided as much as possible, and if they are carried out they should be repaired permanently as soon as possible.

All equipment used in production and packaging must be designed and constructed to prevent contamination, easy to clean and maintain. The objective of hygienic design is to reduce or eliminate the risk that there may be a source of physical, chemical or microbiological contamination for food, both directly and indirectly. In addition, the hygienic design pursues two other purposes such as facilitating cleaning and disinfection and contributing to the conservation and maintenance of the equipment itself or installation. Therefore the concept of hygienic design combines factors of mechanical type, technology and food hygiene. A multitude of factors must be taken into account, such as construction materials, contact surfaces, accessibility, drainability, etc.

> An international standard of reference is BS EN 1672-2: 2005 + A1: 2009 Food Processing Machinery

An international standard of reference is BS EN 1672-2: 2005 + A1: 2009 Machinery for food processing: basic concepts and hygiene requirements, which specifies the common hygiene requirements applicable to machinery for the preparation and processing of food, in order to eliminate or minimize the risk of infection, infection, illness or injury caused by food.

The equipment must meet the principles established in the hygienic design:

- ❖ Surfaces in contact with food should be smooth and accessible and not be a source of contamination and should not contribute to the proliferation of microorganisms.
- ❖ Horizontal surfaces should be avoided, they should slope towards one side, so that the liquid flows away from the area in contact with the food. The surfaces designed to prevent stagnation are predominantly convex and rounded to promote the circulation of liquids.
- ❖ Self-draining. The drainage systems will avoid splashing, they can be easily cleaned and they will have the appropriate inclination to facilitate the effluents outlet.
- ❖ Be compatible with the cleaning agents used.
- ❖ Pipes and ducts must be clean and drainable and not cause condensation or leaks that could contaminate the product.
- ❖ Valves and controls must be safe to prevent contamination.
- ❖ Equipment containing toxic metals should not be allowed.

Management of purchased materials and services.

> Documented information must exist to evaluate, approve and monitor the suppliers in order to ensure compliance with the established requirements.

The purchased materials, services and subcontracted activities that participate in food safety and its packaging must be controlled to ensure that they have the capacity to meet the requirements. The organization must have clarity in the requirements demanded to each one of the suppliers, these should be in a written contract.

Documented information must exist to evaluate, approve and monitor the suppliers in order to ensure compliance with the established requirements. The method used will be justified by risk assessment and risk analysis, including the potential danger of food safety for food packaging.

The provider process should include: The provider's ability to meet the requirements, a description of how the provider is evaluated.

The monitoring includes compliance with agreed specifications, delivery of analysis certificates or quality certificates for each delivery (The CFR 21 part 110, allows to use quality certificates to ensure the quality, safety and safety of the raw material together with a program of Supplier Certification.), Evaluation of HACCP programs, information on the safety of suppliers, compliance with legal requirements and also carry out audits in the facilities of suppliers.

A Supplier Certification Program, includes local and international suppliers, local suppliers must be audited or inspected periodically (a recommendation is at least annually), international suppliers must send documents demonstrating that they have implemented a safety system in place. Its process and facilities and a documentary evaluation of these suppliers must be carried out.

The organization must have a list of approved providers that includes a history of the performance they have been developing.

All incoming raw materials must be inspected, tested or covered by COA / DOC to verify compliance with specified requirements prior to acceptance or use. The verification method must be documented.

Where tamper proof seals are used, a verification process must be established to verify compliance with relevant customer or regulatory requirements.

Measures for prevention of contamination.

The main tool to ensure that sources of contamination are controlled is by performing a hazard analysis, determining the possible sources of microbiological, physical and chemical contamination, and implementing their mitigation measures.

> Mixtures of raw materials, materials, intermediate products, finished product should be avoided to prevent cross contamination.

When necessary according to the hazard analysis, tests of the products must be carried out externally, these must be carried out by an entity that complies with all the regulations required by the regulatory entities and their tests must be certified under the standard ISO 17025.

Mixtures of raw materials, materials, intermediate products, finished product should be avoided to prevent cross contamination.

When samples of raw materials and materials are taken, and this involves direct contact, procedures must be defined to avoid contamination of the products.

When there are reprocesses or products that have been recovered and have not been segregated or handled correctly, they may cause contamination of raw materials, packaging materials, products in preparation and finished products.

Whenever a contamination incident occurs, the cleaning and / or maintenance processes will take place under the activities to carry out the correction and these will be under surveillance by responsible persons designated for such task. After having carried out the cleaning and / or maintenance process, the product that cannot be brought to the established standard must be discarded.

Microbiological Contamination:	Where there is a potential for microbiological contamination, measures must be implemented to prevent or control the hazard.
Physical Contamination:	When glass and brittle plastic are used (in applications related to the productive process and handling, not just lighting) in the production or storage areas, periodic inspection requirements and defined procedures should be established in case of breakage. Glass and fragile materials (such as hard plastic components in the equipment, visors in storage containers) should be avoided where relevant and possible.
	In areas of production and storage, the surfaces intended to have contact with the product must be free of splinters and any other source of contamination. They should be suitable for easy and effective cleaning.
	There must be a formal procedure for the use of "sharp objects". Sharp objects or loose tools will not be left anywhere and on surfaces where product contamination may occur. The use of pressure cutting blades will be prohibited.
	Buildings, facilities and equipment should be cleaned to remove dust, cobwebs, scales and fragments to maintain an acceptable level of cleanliness.
Chemical Contamination:	Printed and coated materials should be handled and stored so that the printed or coated part does not endanger the food, it is not mandatory but these printing and coating inks should be food grade to minimize the risk of contamination.
	Chemical products, including cleaning materials, pest control and lubricants, will be evaluated and controlled to avoid contamination of the product.
	The lubricant intended to come in contact with the product must be of a suitable grade for the intended use.
Chemical Migration:	Where there is a potential danger to food security due to migration or other transfer mechanism, controls should be implemented to prevent or control the hazard. It is advisable to carry out studies of migration of inks from the printed side of the packaging to the non-printed and mandatory if the non-printed side has contact with the

	food. Studies should be conducted if the package does not alter the flavor of the food or alter its composition.
	The packaging (for example, pallets, films, containers and others) must be made of a suitable material and be clean and must not contaminate the food packaging.
Food Allergen Management:	When a potential for contamination by food allergens has been identified, controls to prevent or control hazards should be established, documented and implemented and recorded and labeled accordingly.

Cleaning.

> Cleaning is not only appearance of the facilities, cleaning methods and programs must take into account the safety of food and the analysis of hazards.

Appropriate cleaning programs should be established for specific areas to keep the production equipment and the environment in hygienic conditions. If cleaning activities are subcontracted, the approved supplier will be competent and will maintain the documentation as specified by the organization.

Cleaning is not only appearance of the facilities, cleaning methods and programs must take into account the safety of food and the analysis of hazards.

Organizations must have a master cleaning program that includes all areas and must be done in a preventive manner in order to avoid contamination of raw materials, packaging, machinery, equipment and utensils.

A lot of attention must be paid to the cleaning and sanitizing products used on the surfaces that come in contact with the food.

The cleaning program should contain the following points: areas to be cleaned, equipment and its parts where cleaning is necessary, specific cleaning tasks correctly defined and with those responsible, methods for cleaning and frequency, monitoring and verification of the cleaning efficiency.

The equipment used for the handling of all products -forklifts, elevators, pallet jacks- must be included in the cleaning program.

It is not advisable to use compressed air in the cleaning activities, unless there are two conditions: the pressure is restricted and that we are 100% sure that the finished product, intermediate, in process, raw materials and materials will not be contaminated.

Cleaning methods should include:

- → The chemicals that will be used in each task and its concentration. These chemicals must be properly labeled and when not in use they must be stored away from the processing and storage areas.
- → The equipment and tools used in cleaning tasks. They will be coded by means of colors as an example to be able to differentiate them in the areas that are used according to their intended use. The rags that are used in areas where the food has contacts should not leave residues of the same cloth. If stairs or ladders are used, they must be in good cleaning condition and not be a potential source of contamination.
- → Appropriate clothing. In order that the uniforms and the people who do the tasks are not a source of contamination.

Pest control.

Pest control refers to all those mechanisms carried out for the control or regulation of all those animal species defined as pests or pests, in order to protect individuals and companies from the potential loss of goods or health risks.

> In the control of pests, evaluations, monitoring and management of pest activities must be carried out in order to identify, prevent and eliminate the conditions that may generate or maintain a population of pests.

Pests are a real problem for business; and the regulations of many countries establish that companies have a supplier of pest control, to allow its operation, which includes certifications and regular inspections, which is why hiring a professional in pest control, is not something that Companies can afford to take it lightly.

If the pest control is assigned to an external company, there must be a contract signed between both parties, this will clearly define the responsibilities of the parties regarding the effective management of the pest control program. The external company must have all the regulatory permits that allow it to operate and its personnel must have all the skills and qualifications to perform those tasks.

In the control of pests, evaluations, monitoring and management of pest activities must be carried out in order to identify, prevent and eliminate the conditions that may generate or maintain a population of pests. An annual evaluation of the facility is very important because it provides an assessment of the effectiveness of the pest control program.

The organization must have a designated person to manage and control pest control activities or with designated personnel in this case, expert contractors. Pest management programs must be documented and identify target pests and address plans, methods, schedules, control procedures and, when necessary, staff training requirements.

Programs must include a list of approved chemicals for use in specific areas of the establishment.

The establishment must be kept in good condition. Effective measures must be implemented to prevent pests from entering the establishment. External doors, windows or ventilation openings must be designed to prevent the entry of pests. All external doors must be kept in good condition and closed when not in use.

Materials stored in warehouses if they show signs of being infested will be handled in such a way as to prevent contamination to other materials. The potential refuge of pests must be eliminated. Where external space is used for storage, stored items must be protected from weather and damage caused by pests, in other words there should be no attractive habitat in the facility or in the vicinity of it that increases the chances of having problems of pests.

Pest monitoring programs should include the placement of detectors and traps at key locations to identify pest activity. You must have a map of detectors and traps. The management of external rodent monitoring devices will discourage their entry into the facility. To prevent the entry of pests into the facilities, it is important to create trap circuits and monitor them frequently to evaluate the quantity of pests captured. It is also important to have internal devices for monitoring rodents, which will identify and capture rodents that gain access to the facility. Birds are considered pests that due to their excrement can cause a lot of contamination in the materials. For the control of birds only methods considered legal should be used.

The detectors and traps must be designed and located to avoid contamination of any material. The detectors and traps will be of robust construction and resistant to handling. They will be appropriate for the objective pest. The detectors and traps should be inspected with a frequency that allows identifying new pest activities. Inspection results will be analyzed to identify trends in pest activity.

The eradication measures will be applied immediately after the presence of an infestation is notified. The facility will keep the updated pesticide label of its safety sheets, these products must have regulatory permits for their use. All documentation of these pesticides must be in the language understood by all personnel.

The application of pesticides should be restricted to trained personnel and should be controlled to prevent food hazards for safety. Records of the use of pesticides should be kept to show the type, quantity and concentrations used; where, when and how it is applied; and the objective plague.

Personnel hygiene and facilities.

Personal hygiene and behavior is considered a danger in the safety of food. It will be established that all personnel, visitors and contractors must comply with the documented requirements, comply with the installation policy.

The scope of the points of interest in hygiene is detailed:

Personnel hygiene, changing facilities and toilets:	Personnel hygiene facilities must be available to maintain the degree of personal hygiene required by the organization. The facilities should be located near the points where hygiene requirements apply and will be clearly designated. Provide a suitable number and location of means of washing, drying and, when necessary, hand disinfection. The products to sanitize the hands will be monitored regularly to see if they have the right concentration to ensure their effectiveness. When appropriate, posters will be placed with instructions on "Washing Hands" in toilets and at the entrance of production areas. Provide an adequate number of hygienic services with an adequate hygienic design and sufficiently separated from the production area, each with washing, drying and, when necessary, disinfection facilities. Bathrooms and changing rooms will be kept clean. Have adequate facilities for changing clothes and storage for all personnel working in production, packaging and storage areas. These exchange and storage facilities must be accessible without crossing the production and storage areas when they come from abroad. Personnel lockers, owned by the company, will be inspected at a specified frequency.
Staff canteens and designated eating and smoking areas:	Staff canteens and designated areas for storage, consumption and food preparation must be located and administered in an appropriate manner to avoid contamination of production areas.

	If there is an area where food is prepared, be it by the organization or by an external supplier, you must have the respective permits by the relevant authorities.
	All food, beverages and medications must be stored in the designated areas. Procedures should be established to control the use of medications to prevent product contamination.
	Eating (including consumption of confectionery, chewing gum or chewing tobacco), drinking, other than water and smoking should only be allowed in the designated areas. Where potable water is allowed, it must be subject to control to prevent spills and contamination.
Workwear and protective clothing:	The organization must ensure that personnel working or entering production or storage areas must wear work clothes that are suitable for their purpose, in good condition and that do not present any potential for contamination. Work clothes must be properly segregated from personal clothing. The organization must ensure that the staff keeps their work uniform clean and ensures that there is uniform change daily.
	When appropriate, work clothes or other appropriate protection will provide coverage for the hair, mouth, and beard. Where gloves are used for food packaging, these will be fit for purpose and in good condition.
	Personal protective equipment, when necessary, should be designed to prevent contamination and should be maintained in a hygienic condition.
Illness and injuries:	The facility will have current policies and enforce them to prevent diseases or infections from contaminating the products.
	All injuries, including minor cuts, will be treated promptly and appropriately.
	All personnel health records must be updated and available when required.
Personal cleanliness:	For handwashing, the organization must implement a methodology that includes washing hands before initiating any operation that could jeopardize product safety. After using the health services. Before and after each meal or when deemed necessary.
Personal behavior:	This should be governed by policies and procedures, the activities that represent a risk to the product should be regulated and monitored. This action can be directed by means of signs in each specific area: no smoking, no eating, use of personal protective equipment, no chewing gums, no jewelry use, no nail painted. Keep the lockers free of food, etc.

Rework.

> The organization will designate a specific area for re-processing. The area will be segregated and delimited to avoid mixtures that could alter the traceability of the product.

The rework will be stored, managed and used in a manner that maintains the performance of food safety, quality, traceability and regulatory compliance.

The organization will designate a specific area for re-processing. The area will be segregated and delimited to avoid mixtures that could alter the traceability of the product.

Reprocessing must be maintained at the minimum possible levels and documented information must be maintained on the activities carried out as well as their release.

When rework should be incorporated into the production process, the acceptable quantity, type and conditions of use of rework should be specified. The addition method will be defined, including the necessary pre-processing steps.

Measures must be taken to avoid rework processes that allow raw materials, intermediate products or food packaging to be contaminated with materials not intended for contact with food. Validation records will be saved to demonstrate compliance with regulations and customer requirements. The requirements are maintained following the specified rework process.

Withdrawal procedures.

A product recall is a request to return to the manufacturer a lot or a whole series of a product, usually due to the discovery of security issues or a defect. Once a suspicious product is located, the Withdrawal or Withdrawal Program will outline the procedures for the rapid and controlled removal of the product from the market.

There must be systems in place to ensure that products that do not meet the necessary food safety standards can be identified, located and eliminated from all the necessary points in the supply chain. The system must be registered and tested at an appropriate frequency, the following results will be documented: The traceability of all the materials and ingredients used in the elaboration of the final product that has been removed, the degree of success, the time required to carry out tests.

There must be a documented procedure that specifies: those who are part of the retirement team, such as internal and external communication, how members are contacted outside of working hours, what are the roles and responsibilities of each team member, how can I contact the involved suppliers if there are any. There must be evidence that this procedure is known and available.

Storage and transport.

> All raw materials and materials, intermediate products and packaging materials should be stored and handled in such a way as to avoid contamination such as dust, condensation, fumes, odors and other sources.

All raw materials and materials, intermediate products and packaging materials should be stored and handled in such a way as to avoid contamination such as dust, condensation, fumes, odors and other sources.

The organization must maintain effective controls in storage areas such as temperature, humidity and other environmental conditions that are required for the conservation of raw materials, materials, intermediate and finished products.

Waste and chemicals must be stored separately. The organization must implement measurements to ensure that storage will not jeopardize the safety of the food. Special handling procedures will be followed for packaging materials that present risks to the safety of the product if used improperly (for example, glass or aseptic packaging material). Faults and Corrective Actions will be documented.

If for some reason there is storage on the outside of the facilities, they must be properly protected against deterioration and contamination.

An inventory rotation system should be implemented to ensure that the first ones use the first materials to expire. The dates to facilitate the rotation of inventory will be in a visible place on the platform or the individual container.

Research and Development items and raw materials, packaging material and finished products that are used infrequently will be inspected regularly for contamination indications.

The products returned by customers will not return to the storage area for finished products without having been inspected and released for use by authorized personnel.

Vehicle containers where materials are received or products delivered to customers should be checked before and during the unloading to verify that food safety and safety of raw materials have been maintained during transit.

This revision must include the following points: general condition of the outside of the container, shipping documents, company name and contact, security stamp numbers (these must match those stated in the documents), quantity and batch of materials, compatibility of the transported materials, identification of the driver, presence of holes, unevenness or other defects in the vehicle that allow the entry of contaminants during transport, presence of bad odors from previous transports, deficient sanitary conditions of the container, presence of materials in the floor that have been extended in the container to cover the odors, interior lights covered to minimize cross contamination by broken glass, there should be no presence of pests, correct loading of allergen and non-allergen materials, total presence of cross-contamination of the different materials that are transported.

Security is another important consideration during the download process. During unloading, some seals may have been removed and several points of entry to the tank may be opened for ventilation.

Security seals serve to protect freight transport. The types of safety markers are diverse to meet every need. They are used in boxes of trailers, hoppers, trucks, containers, drums, among other containers. There are four main types: nail (barrel or bottle), cable, plastic and metal. The nail markers are resistant and very durable, consisting of a galvanized steel nail and hard plastic. The cables use a braided steel cable that is versatile and strong. In international trade only safety markers that comply with ISO / PAS 17712 are accepted, this standard requires compliance with the following standards:

- ⇨ Strong and durable to withstand accidental breakage or early deterioration (due to weather conditions or chemical action during handling).
- ⇨ They will have to be identified by a unique brand and number easily readable. Any modification of the brand will cause irreversible destruction of the brand.
- ⇨ They must be constructed in such a way that they cannot be removed without leaving traces or visible traces.
- ⇨ Must be designed to not allow more than its use only once.
- ⇨ They must be designed in such a way that their forgery is difficult.

The area around the unloading area should be controlled to ensure that unauthorized persons do not attempt to access these points. Any dome or hatch that has been opened in the container for ventilation must be equipped with appropriate screens or filters to prevent the entry of contaminants during the loading or unloading process.

After conducting the inspection, all results must be documented on an inspection form and must be signed by the person performing the inspection. The actual conditions of the vehicles and products must be recorded. Any discrepancy, rejected material or rejected charge must be documented. These records must be kept on file for a set period of time. It is also a good idea to keep track of the lot numbers of these materials in order to ensure that they are not discharged to a different vehicle and sent back to the facility. Regulated products may require a specific record retention period. A minimum of two years of record retention is recommended according to the food safety modernization law, for products that are not found under other specific regulations.

Food packaging information and customer communication.

The organization must comply with the food safety requirements demanded by customers and regulations. The organization must obtain the necessary information to determine that the product to be provided is suitable for the intended use. If changes are made to the product or packaging, the organization must ensure that these changes do not jeopardize the safety of the product and promptly inform customers.

The labeling of the product is very important, it carries information of great utility for those who acquire the product and have a description of it.

The Food Codex provides a standard for the labeling and declaration of pre-packaged foods (CODEX STAN 1-1985, Rev. 1-1991).

Food defense and bioterrorism.

Each organization must evaluate the risk for products that represent possible acts of sabotage, vandalism or terrorism and proportional protection measures will be established.

The facility will maintain evidence of registration with the FDA in accordance with the Bioterrorism Act and will renew the records as frequently as defined by the FDA. This requirement will only apply if the facility processes, processes, packages, stores and distributes or exports food for human or animal consumption in the United States.

The bioterrorism program must be documented and with evidence that it is implemented, monitored and, improved according to the findings that are found.

The program must include at least the following points: Periodic review of installation vulnerabilities, prevention of unauthorized entries, transportation and personnel checks, updated references of all personnel, security in all areas of product storage, security of physical and electronic information, safety in transportation and product distribution.

The monitoring of this program must be carried out by trained and competent personnel.

Example of checklist and monitoring of compliance with GMP.

C: Conforming Activity
NC: Non-compliant activity

Area	Activity to verify	C	NC	Comments
Establishment	The areas that delimit the organization of neighbors are in good condition and prevent pollution that may come from sources abroad.			
	Weeds or tall grasses near the facilities.			
	Ceilings are properly maintained: free of dirt, rust, free of leaks, holes, cracks, peeling paint, no condensation.			
	Surroundings free of waste, dust, stagnant water and other pollutants.			
	Drains of roofs and terrains in good condition.			
	External storage of equipment will be minimal and this will be controlled to avoid being a refuge for pests.			
	Easy to clean floors, without cracks, with clean, waterproof joints, with slopes to avoid accumulations of liquids, according to the demand of the type of product.			
	Drains designed to prevent contamination, easy to clean, with grids to prevent entry of pests.			
	Walls in good condition free of holes and cracks that can serve as accumulators of dust and pest shelters.			
	Structures without rust, peeling paint, free of dirt.			
Layout and workspace	There is a separation of the equipment to the wall (sanitary cord) that allows cleaning activities.			
	Sanitary curve between walls and floors, walls and ceilings.			
	Sufficient space that allows flow of materials, products and people through the process.			
	Intentional openings of transfers of products, services, materials are designed to prevent entries of foreign materials.			

Area	Activity to verify	C	NC	Comments
The services used by the operation	The equipment is placed in a way that allows good hygiene, cleanliness and operation.			
	Storage areas provide protection from dust and other sources of contamination.			
	Storage areas are dry and ventilated, their temperature is controlled if required.			
	The materials, products, chemicals are stored in a way that prevents contamination and deterioration. Its storage allows control and cleaning.			
	Chemicals are labeled and safeguarded according to the manufacturer's instructions.			
	The containers to transfer materials are correctly identified.			
	The water for product processing meets the required standards.			
	The water for hand washing is chlorinated.			
	The residual chlorine analyzes are in accordance with local regulations.			
	The different types of water are correctly identified.			
	There are lighting studies at the points where it is required.			
	The luminaries are protected from cracks that could jeopardize the safety of the products.			
	The compressed air system has liquid separator filters (15 microns), coalescing filters (1 to 0.3 microns) and activated carbon filters.			
	There is a ventilation system that removes heat and particles in a controlled manner.			
	The oil in the compressors is food grade.			
Waste management	Deposits are identified to collect waste.			
	These deposits are clean and covered.			
	They are emptied with an established frequency.			
	When containers of products are used to store waste, these containers are free of labels.			
Cleaning and maintenance of equipment	All equipment has hygienic design including tables, chairs and benches.			
	The surfaces that come into contact with the product are easy to clean and do not transfer contaminants to the product.			
	There is a preventive maintenance plan and there is evidence that it is met.			
	Maintenance follows procedures that prevent the product from being contaminated during and after maintenance.			
Management of purchased materials and services	The services that are subcontracted are controlled in order to prevent possible contamination			
	The service providers are aware of the safety requirements that must be met when entering the facilities.			
	The providers are evaluated periodically.			
	All material and product revenues are accompanied by certificates of analysis or compliance.			

Area	Activity to verify	C	NC	Comments
	The transports are verified before the discharges are made.			
	The seals, their status are verified and they are checked against those who report the documents.			
	The characteristics and specifications of all the materials that enter the organization are reviewed.			
Measures to prevent contamination	There is an analysis to verify the physical, chemical and microbiological hazards that may affect the process and the product.			
	Mixed products are observed in warehouse and process areas.			
	After any maintenance activity the contaminated products, if any, are discarded.			
	There is a procedure to identify, control and monitor glass and brittle plastics.			
	There is a procedure to identify, control and monitor the cutting corners.			
	There is an inventory of brittle glass and plastic.			
	There is presence of physical contaminants in walls, floors, hanging structures, roof, and lamps.			
	There is a program for the control of chemical products			
	The organization ensures that the sides of the packaging material that have an impression do not touch the product nor do the contact surfaces eat product.			
	There are studies that show that the migration of inks and solvents does not reach the product.			
	Lubricants that may have occasional contact with the product are of the appropriate grade.			
	Where there is possible contamination of allergens, preventive measures are taken.			
Cleaning	There is a documented master cleaning program known to those responsible.			
	The cleaning program specifies: areas are clean, responsibilities, methods, frequency, monitoring and verification.			
	There are records that show that the cleaning has been carried out.			
	Equipment and cleaning utensils are in good condition.			
	The organization is assured that the cleaning utensils are not a source of cross contamination.			
	Cleaning chemicals are stored according to the manufacturer's instructions.			
	The cleaning program is evaluated in its effectiveness.			
Pest control	There is a pest control program implemented in the organization.			
	There is an annual evaluation of the IPM.			
	The IPM program includes analysis and identification of sources of pests, methods, schedules, procedures, evidence of trained personnel.			
	If the company that provides the service has this regulatory permission to operate.			

Area	Activity to verify	C	NC	Comments
	The chemicals used are approved by the corresponding entities.			
	There are areas that could be refuges for pests.			
	There is a general diagram of where the traps for pests are located.			
	External doors, windows, ventilation holes are designed not to be pest entrances. They are in good condition.			
	There is a periodic monitoring of the traps. They are in good condition. This monitoring is documented.			
	If plagues are detected there are documented corrective actions to eradicate them and their follow-up.			
Hygiene of personnel and facilities	There are separate facilities for men and women.			
	The number of sanitary facilities is in accordance with what is required by local legislation.			
	The sanitary facilities are located in such a way that they are not a potential source of contamination.			
	There is an area for changing clothes with their lockers to store personal items.			
	The lockers are clean without traces of food storage.			
	There are designated areas to consume food.			
	If food is prepared within the organization, it must have the corresponding perms.			
	There is signage indicating the prohibitions of each area.			
	There is a specific area for smokers.			
	There are garbage deposits in different areas. They are closed and in good condition.			
	Workers are provided with the proper work clothing and the correct number of them.			
	Sick staff is observed working on the processes.			
	If a worker becomes ill or injured, he leaves the facility with the permission of his superior.			
	There is a policy that indicates the good behavior of workers within the facilities.			
	The use of jewelry and personal items that may cause contamination to products is prohibited.			
	There is a whole culture of hand washing: before and after eating, when you start your work or when necessary.			
Re work	There is a specific area to do re jobs.			
	It is confined or separated to avoid confusion.			
	The products that have suffered rework are correctly identified.			
	In this area all measures to prevent contamination are implemented.			
	There is documented information on the products that have suffered rework.			

Area	Activity to verify	C	NC	Comments
Product withdrawal procedures	There is a documented product recall program.			
	This program is validated at least once a year.			
	There is a product recall team. Their roles and responsibilities are defined.			
	There are telephone numbers to contact team members, suppliers and customers.			
	There is documented evidence that the program has been validated at least once a year.			
Storage and transport	All materials are confined in the stores.			
	There are mixtures of materials, raw materials, intermediate products and finished products.			
	If the products require them, records of temperature and humidity are kept.			
	Products are observed on the floor without pallets.			
	The pallets are fumigated or have heat treatment.			
	The areas are free of contamination.			
	All chemicals and lubricants are stored separately.			
	An inventory rotation system is implemented.			
	There is a transportation checklist.			
	The pallets are inspected before use to ensure that they are not a source of contamination.			
Product information and communication with customers	The organization can demonstrate that it complies with all the requirements and regulations.			
	There is necessary information to know if the product delivered to customers fulfills its intended use.			
	The organization can ensure that the product information is complete with all that is required.			
	Certificates of compliance are delivered for each delivery of products.			
	Any change of specification, production methods, forms of packaging, formulation, raw materials are informed to the client.			
Food defense and bioterrorism program	There is a documented program for the defense of food.			
	There is a team to protect food			
	There is a methodology to know if your product has been adulterated or falsified.			
	There are vulnerability verification records.			
	There are corrective actions when vulnerabilities are detected.			
	There is an on-site procedure to handle incidents.			
	All the entries and exits of people to the facilities are documented.			
	Confidential information is controlled.			
	There are updated records of all the people who work, enter and leave the organization.			
	The production and storage areas are secured to avoid intruders.			

Glossary.

HACCPC:	Hazard Analysis and Critical Control Points. Preventive system of food safety management applied to the entire food chain, from primary production to retail distribution.
GMP:	Good Manufacturing Practices.
CFR:	Code of Federal Regulations in the United States of America.
Sanitary Cord:	Perimetral cord used for the proper functioning of integrated pest management.
Health Curve:	They are those that go where the walls form an inner edge (inner corner) that is, in the joints of two walls at an angle or also wall-floor, wall-wall and wall-ceiling, in order to facilitate cleaning and avoid the accumulation of bacteria or agents that can produce pathogenic viruses.
Hazardous waste:	Hazardous waste is any solid, pasty or liquid material as well as gaseous contained in containers, which being the result of a process of production, transformation, use or consumption, is intended for abandonment and contains in its composition certain substances in quantities or concentrations such that represent a risk to human health, natural resources and the environment.
FDA:	The Food and Drug Administration (FDA or US FDA) is a federal agency of the Department of Health and Human Services of the United States, one of the federal executive departments of the United States. The FDA is responsible for protecting and promoting public health through the control and supervision of food safety, tobacco products, dietary supplements, prescription and over-the-counter pharmaceutical medications (medicines), vaccines, bio-pharmaceutical products, blood transfusions, medical devices, electromagnetic radiation emitting devices (ERED), cosmetics, food and feed for animals and veterinary products.
Food grade lubricants:	Food grade lubricants are accepted lubricants for use in equipment, applications and processing plants for meat, poultry and other foods. The types of food grade lubricants are divided into three categories based on the likelihood of coming into contact with food. The USDA created the original designation for food grade H1, H2 and H3, which is the terminology in use.
IPM:	Integrated Pest Management Program.
Standard 3-A:	3-A Sanitary Standards, Inc., operates as an independent non-profit corporation. More than 360 companies from the United States and 22 other countries around the world are authorized to display the 3-A symbol on various types of food processing equipment.
WHO:	World Health Organization. Organization of the United Nations (UN) specialized in managing policies of prevention, promotion and intervention in health worldwide. It was initially organized by the Economic and Social Council of the United Nations, which prompted the drafting of the first statutes of WHO.
PRP:	Pre-Requisite Programs required by any standard or scheme. Programs that must be fulfilled.

OPRP: Operational Prerequisite Programs, arise from the analysis of hazards and often also become control measures without becoming critical control points.
COA: Analysis certificate.
DOC: Declaration of conformity.

References.

ISO TS 22002-1: 2009 Programs Pre Requirements in Food Safety - Food Manufacturing.

ISO TS 22002-4: 2013 Programs Pre Requirements in Food Safety - Manufacture of Food Packaging.

About the Author.

CARLOS H HERNANDEZ, Systems Engineer with experience in management of industrial plants and primary plastic packaging in the beverage industries. Post Graduate Studies in Business Administration, Risk Prevention and Project Management. Extensive experience in consulting and implementation of management systems based on ISO Standards, as well as Lead Auditor for ISO 9001, 14001, 22000 and OHSAS 18001 standards, Member of organizations for the improvement of quality and competitiveness, as well as university teacher and business trainer

Otras Publicaciones.

- HACCP Concepts & Quick Reference 1st Ed Eng. 2017.
- Understanding ISO 9001:2015 1st Ed Eng. 2018.

www.ingramcontent.com/pod-product-compliance
Lightning Source LLC
Chambersburg PA
CBHW071158220526
45468CB00003B/1072